Community Helpers at Work

A Day with a Police Officer

By Katie Kawa

New York

Published in 2021 by Cavendish Square Publishing, LLC
243 5th Avenue, Suite 136, New York, NY 10016

Copyright © 2021 by Cavendish Square Publishing, LLC

First Edition

No part of this publication may be reproduced, stored in a retrieval system, or transmitted in any form or by any means—electronic, mechanical, photocopying, recording, or otherwise—without the prior permission of the copyright owner. Request for permission should be addressed to Permissions, Cavendish Square Publishing, 243 5th Avenue, Suite 136, New York, NY 10016. Tel (877) 980-4450; fax (877) 980-4454.

Website: cavendishsq.com

This publication represents the opinions and views of the author based on his or her personal experience, knowledge, and research. The information in this book serves as a general guide only. The author and publisher have used their best efforts in preparing this book and disclaim liability rising directly or indirectly from the use and application of this book.

Library of Congress Cataloging-in-Publication Data

Names: Kawa, Katie, author.
Title: A day with a police officer / Katie Kawa.
Description: First edition. | New York : Cavendish Square, 2021. | Series: Community helpers at work | Includes bibliographical references and index.
Identifiers: LCCN 2019016197 (print) | LCCN 2019018380 (ebook) | ISBN 9781502658258 (ebook) | ISBN 9781502658241 (library bound) | ISBN 9781502658227 (pbk.) | ISBN 9781502658234 (6 pack)
Subjects: LCSH: Police–Juvenile literature.
Classification: LCC HV7922 (ebook) | LCC HV7922 .M474 2021 (print) | DDC 363.2–dc23
LC record available at https://lccn.loc.gov/2019016197

Editor: Katie Kawa
Copy Editor: Nathan Heidelberger
Designer: Andrea Davison-Bartolotta

The photographs in this book are used by permission and through the courtesy of: Cover John Roman Images/Shutterstock.com; p. 5 LightField Studios/Shutterstock.com; p. 7 kali9/E+/Getty Images; p. 9 Epoxychick/Getty Images; p. 11 travelview/Shutterstock.com; p. 13 Yellow Dog Productions/The Image Bank/Getty Images Plus/Getty Images; p. 15 Photographee.eu/Shutterstock.com; p. 17 Nic Neufield/Shutterstock.com; p. 19 © iStockphoto.com/labsas; p. 21 Leonard Zhukovsky/Shutterstock.com; p. 23 Hill Street Studios/DigitalVision/Getty Images.

Some of the images in this book illustrate individuals who are models. The depictions do not imply actual situations or events.

CPSIA compliance information: Batch #CS20CSQ: For further information contact Cavendish Square Publishing LLC, New York, New York, at 1-877-980-4450.

Printed in the United States of America

CONTENTS

Getting Ready	4
Getting Around	8
How Do They Help?	12
Words to Know	24
Index	24

Getting Ready

Police officers have an important job. They help people in their **community**. They work hard to keep people safe. A police officer's day is very busy. They have many things to do!

Police officers get ready for work. They put on their uniform. This is the clothing they wear at work. They also get their tools. A flashlight is one tool they use.

Getting Around

Police cars have **sirens** and colored lights. This makes them easy to spot. People stop when they see a police car with its lights on. They know they need to get out of the way!

Police officers get around their community in different ways. Not all police officers drive cars. Some police officers ride bikes or walk. Other police officers ride horses! Horses help police officers see in big crowds.

How Do They Help?

Police officers keep the roads safe for other people in their community. They stop speeding cars. There are laws that say how fast cars can go. Police officers make sure people follow those laws.

A police officer can help in an **emergency**. They know what to do when something bad happens. They know first aid. This is a way of caring for people who are sick or hurt.

Police officers help kids. Sometimes kids get lost. If this happens, they can look for a police officer. Then, the police officer can help them find their parents. Police officers want kids to feel safe!

Police officers work in many different places. Some police officers work in schools. They keep schools safe. Other police officers work in airports. They help people feel safe when they travel.

Some police officers work together. This is called having a partner. They spend the day with their partner. A dog can be a police officer's partner too. Police dogs are very helpful!

Police officers face danger at work. They catch people who break laws. These people sometimes go to **jail**. Police officers also try to stop bad things from happening in their community. They're very brave!

WORDS TO KNOW

community: An area where people live; a neighborhood.

emergency: An unsafe event that wasn't expected and that calls for action right away.

jail: A place where people are taken to stay when they have broken the law.

sirens: Devices that make a loud warning sound.

INDEX

C
cars, 8, 10, 12

D
danger, 22
dogs, 20

F
first aid, 14

H
horses, 10

K
kids, 16

S
schools, 18
sirens, 8
speeding, 12

U
uniform, 6